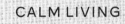
CALM LIVING

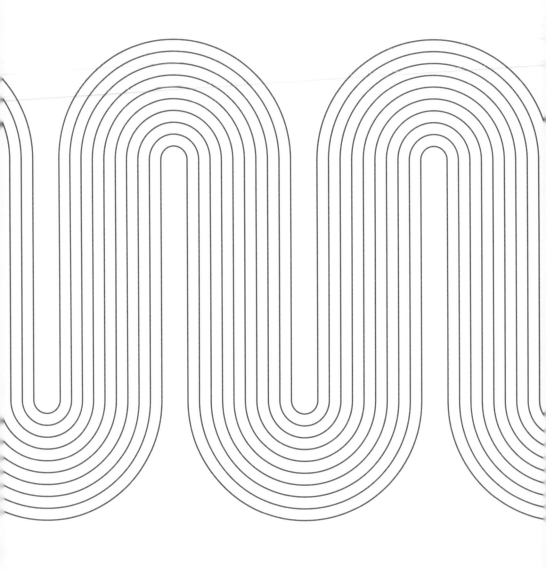

CHRONICLE BOOKS
SAN FRANCISCO

Calm Living

Simple Design Transformations
to Fill Your Spaces with Tranquility

By Olga Trusova

Library of Congress Cataloging-in-Publication Data
Names: Trusova, Olga, author.
Title: Calm living : simple design transformations to fill your spaces with
tranquility / by Olga Trusova.
Description: San Francisco : Chronicle Books, [2023]
Identifiers: LCCN 2022037912 | ISBN 9781797218526 (hardcover)
Subjects: LCSH: Interior decoration--Psychological aspects.
Classification: LCC NK2113 .T78 2023 | DDC 747--dc23/eng/20220822
LC record available at https://lccn.loc.gov/2022037912

Manufactured in China.

Design by **VANESSA DINA**.
Typesetting by **FRANK BRAYTON**.

10 9 8 7 6 5 4 3 2 1

Chronicle books and gifts are available at special quantity discounts to
corporations, professional associations, literacy programs, and other
organizations. For details and discount information, please contact our
premiums department at corporatesales@chroniclebooks.com or at
1-800-759-0190.

Chronicle Books LLC
680 Second Street
San Francisco, California 94107
WWW.CHRONICLEBOOKS.COM

DEDICATED TO LILY

Nothing is a mistake. There's no win and no fail. There's only make. As I entered the Stanford d.school—a design school that changed my life—I noticed a huge black-and-white vertical sign hanging from the ceiling with this famous quote by Corita Kent, an artist and educator, who wrote ten rules for students and teachers to free the creative spirit. I was instantly enamored by this fundamental message and the surrounding creative space, to the point of wanting to replicate it for myself.

We all crave a little space for ourselves, personal space in which to express ourselves and do our best work. Yet our lives, and the spaces we occupy, are filled with hundreds of objects that represent decisions that were never about supporting or inspiring our spirit. You probably have heard of Maslow's hierarchy of needs, often portrayed as a pyramid with the most basic needs for food and shelter at the bottom and self-actualization needs at the top, but do you know he added aesthetics—the appreciation of your surroundings—to the list? Living in a space you find pleasing both physically and emotionally is more than a luxury; it can define who you are and change you for the better.

The desire to create an oasis at home has become more apparent as many people shift to working from home. As we spend increasing amounts of time at home, we put additional requirements and strain on the household. Our spaces have become multifunctional—a family room might have to function as an office, a gathering area, a playroom, and so on. The need for a personal space has also increased; we seek to decompress and reset in the sanctuary of our home. But how do you intentionally carve out a little space for yourself?

Before attending d.school, I studied computer science and built a career working for tech companies in Silicon Valley, writing code. Like many others with a similar background, I struggled to find meaning in my work yet felt guilty about leaving it behind. I liked talking to people and making things with my hands—tinkering and experimenting—which my job did not fulfill. As I sat in a drab cubicle in a generic brown building—one of many—on our original Menlo Park campus, I felt the need to change my environment and my life.

I thought of a friend I had met on a recent trip to Italy, Cristina Bowerman, an editor of art textbooks turned Michelin-star chef, and her theater set designer and restaurateur husband who became her long-term collaborator. Cristina successfully translated her talents into a career in the culinary arts, creating beautiful Italian dishes at Glass Hostaria, a restaurant—designed by her husband—with floors and a ceiling made entirely out of glass in Rome's Trastevere neighborhood. I was jealous.

Sensing my restlessness, my boss at the time asked if I was interested in learning more about interaction design, an emerging field that he believed could build on my knowledge base and provide a new creative outlet. The person who coined the term was teaching at Stanford—and, a year later, I found myself there as one of his students. That year, the d.school was founded. The d.school is dedicated to a human-centered approach to problem solving called design thinking, with an emphasis on uncovering human needs.

Around that time I also had an opportunity to visit the renowned National Institute of Design (NID). The school is located in Ahmedabad, Gujarat, a city with a rich history of craftsmanship and considered the textiles capital of India. In contrast to the contemporary, spare aesthetic of many professional buildings in Silicon Valley, I found a lush green field with students sitting on the ground, painting and drawing, peacocks freely wandering, and a professor dressed in a long kurta reclining by a hundred-year-old tree. It was a memorable, creative setting, so different from what I thought a design school should look like based on my previous experiences. Since that visit, I've studied how different environments, cultures, norms, and rituals foster deliberation and calm. My conclusion is that there is no single aesthetic, but there are underlying principles that can empower anyone to create spaces that bring out the best in themselves and others.

After graduate school, I became a design consultant for Fortune 500 companies and built centers for innovation and creativity around the world. I developed strategies for bringing human-centered design into the workplace, explored the future of work and mobility, and created pathways for employees to be more creative. The insights and learnings I'm sharing with you here are based on my design consulting work, and what I learned at the d.school.

In this book, I will introduce you to the foundational principles of designing a space—whether it's a small apartment, an office, or a large house—that gives you peace and clarity (even amid chaos), enables your mind to flow, and gives you room to learn and grow effortlessly. It isn't about sparse white rooms where everything is in its place; it is about filling your space with intention. Calm is not static.

The concepts in this book are rooted in research but easy to apply in your own space, and you don't need formal training in design to use them. This book will show how simple changes can make any room—and its inhabitants—more inspired. It is a way to care for yourself by addressing an overlooked yet powerful aspect of our lives: our space. More and more people are beginning to understand that space goes hand in hand with how we feel.

One thing I've learned is that the aesthetics of calm do not fit into one mold. An important part of this book is identifying ways that physical spaces and objects can be part of your unique, active tool sets. You'll experiment with physical spaces and ephemeral details, such as day-to-day routines, as a way to practice taking control of the world around you and designing meaningful experiences for yourself and others.

In each chapter of the book, I include short exercises you can do in your space to start to transform your daily experiences. These exercises are an important part of the experience: some require a few minutes of brainstorming, and others require putting down the book and taking on a specific task.

Calm Living will help you create an environment where you feel calm, think clearly, and breathe. These pages are designed to move you from inspiration to action, giving you confidence to tinker with your space and achieve the outcomes you want for and from yourself. Simple, intentional changes to your environment can have a profound impact on your calm and well-being.

—Olga

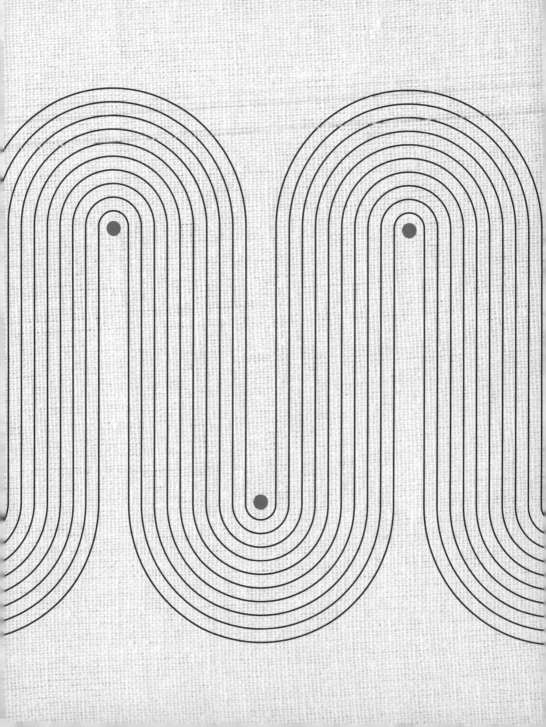

PART ONE

Designing for Calm

WHAT IS CALM AND HOW TO BE THE DESIGNER OF YOUR SPACE

Close your eyes and imagine sitting in a hot tub at night surrounded by the lush greenery of a beautiful island, with the Milky Way spread above your head in the dark sky, a warm breeze caressing your face, the smell of ocean waves crashing on the shore, the sound of palm trees swaying back and forth . . . Do you feel calm? I certainly do. When I talk about calm in this book, this is the kind of feeling I want to evoke. Being calm has been described as being peaceful, quiet, and free from disturbance. When your mind is free and relaxed, rather than feeling anger or anxiety, it allows for greater clarity, a tranquility of sorts. More poetically, a calm sea or a lack of wind represents a certain freedom from rough motion—stillness, serenity. This is the feeling I want you to create in your space to nurture your body, mind, and soul.

A former classmate, Akari, had a spectacular career in technology, as did her husband, Tom. In addition to their successful Silicon Valley jobs, Akari and Tom—both very ambitious, persistent, and committed—also built a wonderful home, family, and community in California's Bay Area. But when their daughter, Sky, turned ten, they suddenly decided to move to Maui. They'd experienced a certain amount of burnout after spending endless hours commuting and never having enough time for what mattered to them—like close relationships or hobbies. Finally, when their daughter started to show serious signs of anxiety from academic and social pressures, they decided to take a monthlong break in Hawaii, where Tom's father had retired. That month was so rejuvenating for the entire family—with paddleboarding, whale watching, soaking up the sun, and swimming in warm ocean water—that they decided to come back for three months next time.

Lo and behold, three months turned into a year. They rented a place and switched to working remotely. Sky enrolled in a local school. Once the opportunity came up to buy a plot of land in an area called the Upcountry, they took it. When I visited them several years later, I drove up to a beautiful hilly area of Maui called Makawao—the cowboy country where the fog settles and cows graze on the dark green hills. Akari and Tom built a beautiful, contemporary house where indoors and outdoors flowed seamlessly. Akari, originally from Japan, incorporated her favorite Japanese design elements into the coastal aesthetics of her new home. Through the sliding glass doors, the living room opened up to a lovely outdoor pool and hot tub. "You can see the Milky Way at night from here," Akari said. As I sat in the hot tub and looked up at the sky, I felt at peace.

When I asked Akari what inspired her to build this house from scratch and make certain design choices with the architects and designers who were helping her, she said it was her childhood in a small Japanese town outside Kyoto, as well as the design school we had both attended. She wanted to give her daughter a carefree childhood running around barefoot among fruit trees and being one with nature, like the one she had in Japan. To accomplish this goal, she applied a design process we learned in school to create a nurturing environment for her family that both inspired and soothed the senses.

The basis of "design thinking," the process Akari used to design her home, is that anyone can approach problems like a designer, being intentional, creative, and collaborative. By applying the core principles of design thinking to the physical environment, you can reimagine your surroundings and create a refuge that nourishes the spirit. Let's take a close look at three crucial elements that—along with such important factors as process, method, and physical design, which we will cover in later chapters—will help you successfully build a calm and supportive environment.

1. **A PROTOTYPING MINDSET.** Everything around us is designed, everyone is a designer, and we can and should tinker with the world to encourage more calm in our lives. You can prototype pretty much anything, even if you're not a trained designer. A prototype is an early sample, model, or release of a product built in order to test a concept or be replicated or learned from. Prototypes can be of physical objects, services, or experiences. You can build to think, to learn, or to test. There are no mistakes; there are only prototypes we can learn from and iterate.

2. **THE RIGHT INTENTIONS.** Setting the right intentions before you begin a project is extremely important for evaluating future outcomes. How do you want to feel when you complete the project? What actions will you be taking? Who will be there with you? You need to be mindful and intentional when designing.

3. **EXPERIENCE DESIGN.** We are designers of our own experiences, and we can play around with the variables we have control over in our lives, such as our immediate surroundings and personal interactions. Space should support the types of behaviors and activities we want to encourage. Space needs to fit our lives and work—not the other way around, where we try to fit into spaces with limitations.

These foundational principles of design thinking helped Akari, and they can help you too—help you create a space that nurtures the body, mind, and soul. In this book, we will be uncovering how to start from a clean slate, as well as how to balance, center, and activate your calm at home—be it a small apartment, a single-family house, or a live-work studio. Designing for calm involves cultivating a prototyping mindset (taking semipermanent steps as a way toward a more refined solution), setting the intention for your space to be a rejuvenating environment, and ultimately being in control of your own experiences at home.

ATTRIBUTES
OF A CALM
ENVIRONMENT

Coming from the Stanford d.school, where the emphasis is on uncovering human needs before generating ideas and building proto-types, and Design for Change (a global move-ment to empower communities to design solutions to difficult problems), I was excited about deep-diving into customers' worlds to seek new insights and opportunities. You need to get out of the building and talk to actual people—your customers—if you want to create something meaningful, delightful, and groundbreaking for them. My former profes-sor, David Kelley—cofounder of IDEO and the d.school—taught his students the value of human-centered design. He said that empathy is the key to unlocking our creative potential to solve difficult challenges. Talking to people is how you understand desirability.

How might we help Viña Santa Rita—a small winery in Chile—scale its operations to support global demand? How might we support winery workers as the business grows? How might we provide robust technology in remote places to enable scale without sacrificing quality? These are some of the questions a design team asks before diving into interviews with customers. The first step in providing something of value to winery workers is gaining empathy for them by putting ourselves in their shoes to observe their environment and uncover unanticipated needs. This critical step lies at the heart of human-centered design.

Design thinking is a tool my classmates and I embraced in different ways to advance the notion of human-centered design in our personal lives and within the different organizations we ended up working for. It begins with gaining empathy for someone, followed by brainstorming a large number of possible

solutions, then rapidly prototyping and testing them with potential users. It is a highly
iterative, circular process that yields products and services that people actually need
and want to use. It is the undercurrent of
this book and what will enable you to design
human-centered environments anchored in
real needs and inspired by radically new ideas.

To think like a designer, consider the eight design abilities that practitioners and academics focus on:

(1) navigate ambiguity,

(2) learn from others (people and contexts),

(3) synthesize information,

(4) rapidly experiment,

(5) move between concrete and abstract,

(6) build and craft intentionally,

(7) communicate deliberately,

(8) and design your design work.

These abilities allow us to apply design thinking in a nonlinear fashion to problems in a variety of settings—from helping a small winery in Chile or a large enterprise like IBM to designing your own life and career. Consider the list above and note which abilities feel natural to you and which ones feel like areas for growth.

Over the last decade, more and more large companies, small businesses, and individuals have embraced human-centered design principles popularized by the world-renowned design firm IDEO and its sister organization, the Stanford d.school. There are corporate clubs and informal meetups sprouting up with the goal of fostering the culture of creativity. As part of my consulting work, I belong to one such cross-company club, along with colleagues from Nordstrom, Fidelity Investments, Hyatt, and JetBlue. We want to empathize with our customers, coworkers, and peers in other companies who also practice innovation in a human-centered way. What do these companies have in common? Fidelity, JetBlue, Hyatt, and Nordstrom all care deeply about customer experience.

For example, I think of Nordstrom as a one-hundred-year-old start-up; it's currently working on creating a new virtual retail experience for its millennial shoppers comparable to its famous personal shopping assistants in its brick-and-mortar stores. To achieve this goal, the Nordstrom innovation team follows methods from human-centered design. A few years ago, I had an opportunity to tour Nordstrom's fantastic Customer Experience Center with them. This space, inside a nondescript South Seattle warehouse, features a replica of a retail store, complete with clothes and a checkout counter. Here, the innovation team can prototype complete shopping experiences before moving them to actual stores. It serves as a safe place for rapid experimentation with physical layouts and new technologies, and learning from others before committing to a particular setup.

Another example comes from the San Francisco Museum of Modern Art (SFMOMA), and it couldn't be more different. From 2013 to 2016, the museum was undergoing a massive redesign and expansion. In anticipation of closing its doors for more than two years, museum leadership engaged the d.school to reimagine a museum outside its walls. Our task was to find a way to extend it beyond the physical space, which wasn't going to be available for a while. What was the core of what SFMOMA provided to its visitors? Could there still be a museum experience when there was no building?

After spending hours observing visitors at SFMOMA, interviewing them, and doing analogous research (looking at similar environments), we landed on several concepts that we ended up prototyping and testing before presenting to the museum leadership: from physically extending the museum (such as artwork pop-ups in other local museums and displaying

31

reproductions or prints in construction under-passes) to offering new online experiences to visitors worldwide (through a virtual museum and mobile apps). In order to support the project's goals, you need to understand who will be using the space and why, prototyping a variety of ideas before landing on the most delightful experience.

Will you be designing, displaying, or selling products, talking to customers, trying out new services, demonstrating, pitching, or doing something else? How will the space support these activities in the current setup? An intentionally designed space enables certain behaviors and actions. The key mindsets you want to encourage should be reflected in the physical environment, where the creative work will be taking place. Space should support and encourage the kinds of activities and actions that will be performed in it: brainstorming, collaborating, prototyping, testing, storytelling, presenting, displaying art or other objects, teaching, performing, studying, and so on.

Imagine yourself as an experience designer working with multiple variables that influence how you interact with your environment—even if it's just a corner of your home. You don't have to be an architect or an interior designer to carve out some space that supports and encourages your creative spirit; you can start by tweaking a few simple things—such as standing while you work to help you generate more ideas or bringing a pet to the office to de-stress—before deep-diving into a more elaborate space redesign project.

For example, in my recent experimental pop-up class on the basics of experience and environments design, co-taught with Scott Witthoft—coauthor of *Make Space: How to Set the Stage for Creative Collaboration*—we had students tease out several universal principles for designing first-time experiences that are important to take into consideration as you embark on your own project. Here are some rules for creating a successful first-time experience:

> Every first-time experience (EFTE) should have some unexpected reward.
>
> EFTE should be completely immersive.
>
> EFTE should stretch out the moment of anticipation.
>
> EFTE should make guests feel authentically immersed.
>
> The outcomes of EFTE should be learned through action.
>
> The excitement of EFTE should be maintained by all subsequent experiences.

EFTE should enhance any positive emotions that people bring to the experience and mitigate any negative ones.

As you continue to design your space, whether it's at home, work, or both, you'll need to think about several other factors; for instance, in the business environment: knowledge sharing across silos, physical spaces with visible project progress, areas for quick experimentation, pop-up studios for quick experiments. You will also have to strategize long-term about how that space will support you as your work grows.

In a 2018 study conducted at Stanford University, twenty-seven design educators were asked to identify all the variables they control in order to create a learning experience for their students. One of the main takeaways was that these teachers often manipulate quite a large number of variables. They explicitly identified more than twenty-five aspects, including where people meet, the size of the team, the tone of the room, and the layout of the physical space.

A SHORT LIST
OF ENVIRONMENTAL
VARIABLES
DESIGN INSTRUCTORS
MANIPULATE

VARIABLE	NUMBER OF PARTICIPANTS WHO GENERATED IT
FACULTY/INSTRUCTORS	18
SPACE (PHYSICAL SPACE, FURNITURE LAYOUT)	16
FRAMING AND SCOPING THE PROJECT GOALS	16
TIME (DURATION OF ACTIVITIES)	14
TEAM (SIZE AND MAKEUP OF TEAM)	13
DELIVERABLES (FORM THE FINAL OUTCOME TAKES)	12
CONNECTION WITH CAMPUS AND COMMUNITY	8
LOCATION (WHERE THE EXPERIENCE HAPPENS)	6
FEEDBACK/CRITIQUE (WHO GIVES IT AND HOW IT IS FRAMED)	6
FUN	5

Although this work was done with educators, it is relevant beyond the classroom for two reasons. One is that the primary job of the educators was to create an environment where people can do creative work. The second is that only two of the variables are uniquely geared to an educational context. The main point is space, which is almost as important as faculty and instructors in this case. Since environment is such an important aspect of our home, study, and work lives, the question is then "What makes a calm environment?" I offer three primary requirements: (a) it soothes the senses, (b) it promotes balance, and (c) it makes life easier. As we move through the rest of his book, I'll be sharing how these attributes can be leveraged to create a calm environment in your space.

SETTING THE RIGHT INTENTIONS FOR YOUR SPACE

Remember Glass Hostaria—the Italian restaurant I mentioned in the introduction? When my friend Cristina met her future husband, Luciano, she was hoping to get a job as a chef at his restaurant in Trastevere. It was a traditional osteria, serving simple food and wine, with a short menu of local specialties, like pasta. As soon as Cristina stepped into the osteria, she realized it wasn't the vision she had in mind of a creative place where traditional dishes were made with local ingredients but given a modern twist. It looked too old-school, and the atmosphere wouldn't complement her cooking style. Similarly, Luciano had a different vision for the small restaurant he'd just bought—with his background in theater set design, he imagined a light and airy place filled with glass, instead of the dark, drab, outdated restaurant it was.

After they became a couple, they sat down and each wrote a few newspaper headlines from the future describing what their restaurant would be famous for and worked backward to create a plan that would achieve the desired outcome. Ultimately, Cristina and Luciano set the intention of creating a state-of-the-art theatrical experience with a fabulous dinner for visitors and locals.

Intentions Tool Kit

The following exercises will help you imagine the possibilities for your space and connect with your design needs and desires so that you can move forward with intention and clarity.

1. The exercise that Cristina and Luciano leveraged as they were planning out their space redesign is called Headlines. It's a useful tool borrowed from marketing and design thinking that enables you to "headline your future" with as much detail as possible, imagining future possibilities, and then work on an action plan for making those headlines a reality. In one short sentence, write a newspaper headline from the future for how you would like your space to feel a year from now. What would that headline emphasize? What do you want from your space? How would you describe it? Reflect on your space requirements and desires.

2. If you're unsure of what headline to write, another fun exercise to try is called Magic Wand. Imagine you have a magic wand that can fix or change anything in your space. What are the top three things you'd like to improve and why? Immerse yourself in your environment, leverage the power of observation, and look with fresh eyes: "I've seen this a million times, but it feels like the first time I'm seeing it!" Look around your space,

don't overthink it, and list your top items in order of priority.

3. The last tool I'd like to suggest is creating an Empathy Map for yourself. Mapping key experiences you're having in your environment on a simple two-by-two matrix aids in redesigning your space to support how you want to feel in it in the future. Draw a grid with four quadrants, with Say and Do in the left column and Think and Feel in the right. Now list how you feel in your space (emotions), what you think about it (thoughts), what you normally do there (actions), and what you say about it to others (descriptions). Does anything stand out as an immediate pain point? How about anything that brings you joy? With a red marker, circle key pain points; with a green one, circle any highlights, or things that are working well that you would like to keep or amplify.

say | think

do | feel

observed < · · · · · · · · · · · · · · · > inferred

Simple yet meaningful exercises like these are meant to help you identify what is most critical to focus on and what you'd do in your dream scenario. Creating boundaries or constraints from the beginning and defining certain design parameters to work with is what designers call *framing*. You need to frame the problem area properly so that you can solve for the right opportunity. It can be overwhelming, not to mention emotionally charged, to think and plan out changes in your space. Framing a challenge in one sentence, a top-three list, or a two-by-two grid forces you to focus.

To conclude Cristina and Luciano's story, Glass Hostaria now boasts a modern design with a play on light, inventive decor, and innovative cuisine. The dining room is clean and modern, built with glass, wood, and metal materials. It matches the elaborate dishes lovingly prepared by the chef while creating a memorable dining experience for the visitors. The restaurant earned a Michelin star for molecular gastronomy—Cristina is one of the few Italian female chefs to receive the award.

Setting the right intentions is extremely important, but you don't have to start big and be overly ambitious too quickly. Your first goal shouldn't be to have your home profiled in Apartment Therapy. Before you begin changing yourself, your space, or the way you act in that space, you need to take stock of what makes you feel most stuck—building on the Empathy Map exercise. B. J. Fogg, a behavioral scientist at Stanford University, calls it cultivating *tiny habits* and suggests starting with brushing one tooth before committing to brushing all your teeth every night. Starting with tiny improvements prevents you from getting overwhelmed by too much change at once.

Remember that you can make any space more conducive to calm through small changes with big impact. For example, you can change your environment by creating intentional areas for inspiration, exploration, and creativity. Don't think of your space in terms of fixed categories: living room, office, bedroom, etc. Instead, consider your space(s) in terms of creative combinations that can serve multiple purposes depending on situations, people, and contexts. You can remix the space around you to create a more dynamic environment.

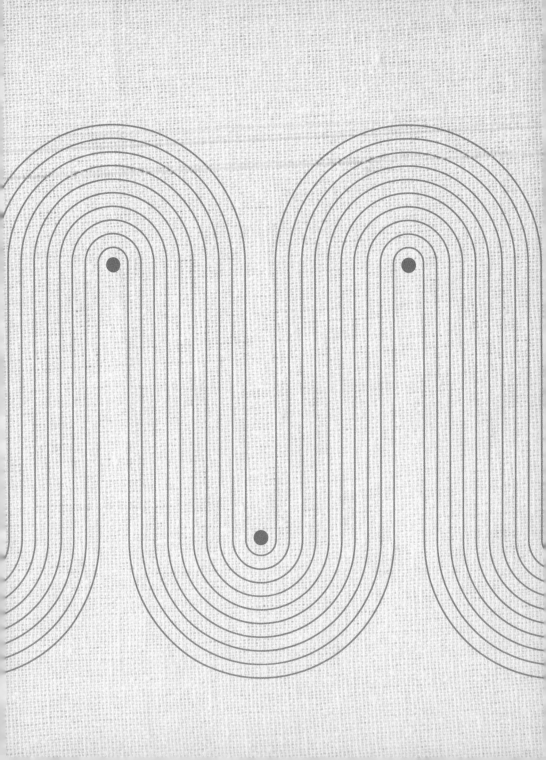

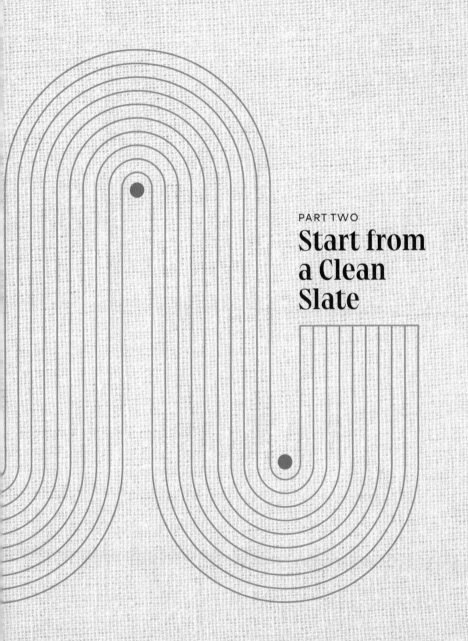

PART TWO

Start from a Clean Slate

PREPARE YOUR SPACE FOR ACTIVITY

Designers build prototypes to think and learn. Gaining the confidence to tinker or prototype like a designer enables you to be more creative and frees you to try new configurations in your space. You can sketch with permanent markers on sticky notes, create mock-ups with cardboard, rapidly prototype with physical objects, or "fake" or create "make-believe" experiences using a concept called "the Wizard of Oz." This act of "making" is a way to try out new ideas before committing to a permanent solution.

Prototyping is about making your idea real with simple and often cheap materials in as short an amount of time as possible. It allows you to try out various design solutions before committing to them. To prepare your space for activity, you can leverage existing objects in your space— desk, chairs, walls, rugs—and determine how they can come alive to support you. Once you identify what you want to do in your home, you can activate it. After all, objects are just objects. It's what we do with them that counts.

You can create different kinds of prototypes for different reasons. Low-fidelity prototypes, such as hand sketches, are fast and enable more iterations and quick feedback. High-fidelity prototypes are great persuasive tools that enable more in-depth feedback and interactions. In this book, we will focus on low-fi prototyping. You can build to think, test, and iterate a specific idea (and to co-design with others). You can prototype just about anything!

Let me share a few radically different examples of prototypes to illustrate how we can use them in our settings. The design firm IDEO was working with a group of doctors, designers, and engineers on the next generation of complex surgical instruments. Everyone was sitting around the table, offering lots of ideas and ultimately not being able to come to any agreement. One surgeon had an idea for a sleek handheld device that he was trying to describe to everyone, when an IDEO designer picked up a few simple prototyping materials and put together a prototype. The designer asked, "Do you mean something like this?" The surgeon exclaimed, "Exactly like this!" After many iterations of the product, this early prototype has become a real surgical instrument.

In addition to creating physical prototypes, you can prototype experiences. A design team at Virgin Atlantic airlines created an experiential prototype by flying its executives to one location and "losing" their luggage. It forced the executives to go down to baggage claim, wait in line, fill out forms, look up information, etc. This was a way to demonstrate what Virgin Atlantic customers have to deal with when they lose their bags and to subsequently inform the redesign of that experience. You can also create paper and digital prototypes for apps, online tools, and complex systems. As designers, we often build to think, learn, and decide: physical prototypes (what something will work like), experiential (what it will feel like), and digital (how it interacts).

Energy of Analogous Spaces

To find and implement inspiration from other spaces and environments, follow these steps:

1. Conduct analogous research.

> Make a list of ten activities that make you feel calm: drinking a warm cup of coffee, watching the sun set, or visiting a museum. Then next to each activity identify the specific environment you associate with the activity. This could include the sounds, smells, colors, quality of light—whatever you can think of.

> Take photos or videos of those environments (if you can), and borrow elements that you can translate in your own space. A design team at Fidelity Investments went through this exercise when they wanted to understand what makes family conversations about finance difficult or uncomfortable and how to make them easier. They decided to first investigate why intimate conversations happen in places such as barbershops and bars by visiting those locations, observing what typically happens when a client shares personal information, and interviewing barbers and bartenders to get their insights about what makes those places good for sharing deeply personal details.

2. Prototype it. You can prototype pretty much anything, even if you're not a trained designer. Prototypes can be of physical objects, services, or experiences. Here is some guidance to get you started:

> For the next two weeks, change something about your space every day to see how you feel. Pick ideas from your list, starting with your low-hanging fruit (the easiest to implement), darling (the most delightful idea), and moon shot (a long-term project).

> Write down your experiment and how it makes you feel each day.

> Keep or toss? Make the change semipermanent.

> Take photos or short videos of your prototypes or space changes.

3. Iterate. Make at least one change to your prototype based on what you've learned from building it.

> You should continue to reassess how these design experiments make you feel in your space. By playing around with or prototyping different arrangements, you can adjust your space and boost how you feel.

KEEP COMFORT WITHIN REACH

As kids we often relied on our favorite stuffed animals, cuddly toys, or blankets for comfort, soothing, and calm—whether before bedtime, during long car rides, or in an emotionally difficult moment. These aids created an opportunity for us to transfer certain feelings over, decompress, or de-escalate a situation, and almost instantly transform our environment—whether it was in bed, in a car, or on a playdate—into a more joyful, peaceful one.

Liz Walsh, a good friend who comes from a sports family and whose father was a coach, just like mine, had recently moved from San Francisco to Los Angeles with her husband and daughter, Ida. Liz of course was dearly missed by her family and friends, myself included, but she wasn't very far—a long drive or a short plane ride away. Ida's grandmother remained in Northern California, and Liz decided to schedule a regular visit when the whole family would drive up the coast from Los Angeles to San Francisco. The drive usually took six to seven hours, and although the ocean views were amazing, it was hard for her three-year-old to sit through.

A gray stuffed bunny rabbit named Fluffy—a hand-me-down from Liz—became Ida's sole consolation and comfort. So every couple of months, Liz, her husband, Ida, and Fluffy got in the car and drove up to see Ida's grandmother. Fluffy remains in their family to this day and travels with them extensively.

Object attachment is the experience a person has when they feel an emotional attachment to an inanimate object. Studies have shown that up to 70 percent of young children in the Western world develop strong attachments to objects such as toys or blankets. In one such study, conducted by Bruce Hood of the University of Bristol and Paul Bloom of Yale University, it was found that children preferred their cherished comfort blankets or favorite teddy bear over duplicates identical in every way—to no surprise of most parents.

Now that we're adults, why not leverage these types of positive attachment objects to create a calmer and healthier environment? Look around your space and you'll discover that you already keep certain comfort items within reach. Perhaps it's your favorite throw on the couch, cozy slippers you put on after a bath, a lucky sweater, or a silly coffee mug you prefer over all others. Many adults already own a favorite thing to which they feel emotionally attached, whether for aesthetic, sentimental, or spiritual reasons.

Aesthetic Value

Some of these attachment objects have aesthetic purposes: they appeal to our senses. In my living room, I put up a few paintings of seascapes that bring calm and serenity to my mind every time I look at them, mentally transporting me to nature as if I were near water, my default happy place. A friend, Beti, loves her Hasami ware—a type of Japanese porcelain with a four-hundred-year history. Clean, simple, and functional plates, mugs, and bowls look modern yet traditional. Beti first discovered Hasami porcelain while working at Apple, where she was gifted a set of stackable tea mugs and small plates for a work anniversary. She instantly fell in love with their simple yet beautiful look, as well as their functional and aesthetically pleasing design. Sipping tea from such a mug gave her instant joy and a moment of happiness each day.

One way to discover your own version of the Hasami mug is by scouting for new designers and designs online, such as on Pinterest—a website full of inspiring mood boards and links. Look for new ideas and suggestions, "like" them, and arrange them into a mood board based on themes: favorite small kitchen items that include interesting creamer jars or salt-cellars, terra-cotta plant pots with different patterns, or even clothes stands. The site provides recommendations based on what you liked, and you might find some new and surprising things as you browse.

Or better yet, get out of your house and go on an expedition looking for some new items that'll bring you comfort. Put on your walking shoes, bring a smartphone for taking photos and notes, and head out to a few boutique furniture and accessories stores. Notice what objects speak to you, draw you in, give you

a positive vibe—but don't buy anything yet.
Spend a few days just exploring before settling
on a new attachment object that aesthetically
pleases you and provides comfort.

Sentimental Value

Sentimental attachment, on the other hand, is often placed on objects that are linked with a core memory about an important event or person. According to a recent study conducted by Mary E. Dozier and Catherine R. Ayers on object attachment published in *Current Opinion Psychology*, "if an older adult believes that they will forget aspects of their family life when they had young children, they may believe that they need to keep all their children's artwork from school. Or, they may want to remember their military service and thus, keep items associated with it for fear they will forget."

Some people keep such sentimental items in a box stored away in an attic, while others display them in a shrine of sorts. I would encourage you to experiment with displaying your sentimental items, almost gallery-like, instead of hiding them away in storage. Your items could go on top of a sideboard in the living room, on the wall, or on a mantel above the fireplace.

One easy way to showcase photos, artwork, papers, etc. that'll save you some horizontal space is to use a cork bulletin board with pushpins. This leverages the walls instead of creating more clutter somewhere else. This way you'll have a chance to experience positive emotions every time you walk by or look at your sentimental items of choice.

Spiritual Value

Leveraging attachment objects for spiritual purposes often involves a certain set of beliefs and rituals. For example, creating a tea ceremony can satisfy the spiritual purposes of reflection, slowing down, and being in the moment. Building on cultural or spiritual traditions within your family lineage, you can intentionally pick out certain items for calm and comfort, then attach a positive routine to them to create more meaningful and joyful experiences in your home.

Using scents is another lovely way to create a mindful ritual and infuse your space with calm. We often focus on visual input when we think of design, but aromatherapy—the practice of using scents for relaxation, restoration, energy, and more—adds another dimension to calm living. Adding your favorite essential oils to a humidifier, burning incense, or lighting a scented candle can transform a room or corner into a small sanctuary. Experiment with what scents make you feel most relaxed.

When using incense or any cleansing herbs or woods, I encourage you to do some research about the sustainability of the materials to ensure that you are buying things from ethical and sustainable sources.

Putting It All Together

To keep comfort within reach, we may rely on attachment objects to soothe our senses, like a Hasami tea mug, or evoke a pleasant memory, like a display of kids' artwork, or we may develop a routine, like lighting candles on a Friday night, to bring warmth and light into our home. The aim is to create comfort and calm in your home with intention and dedication. Every room should feature at least one thing that gives you comfort: an easy chair you can sink into, a soft throw blanket, photos of loved ones, objects you want to touch, objects that hold meaning.

AIM FOR MANAGED COMPLEXITY

An empty room can feel cold and impersonal, while too much clutter adds to stress. The key is to impose order on objects. One way to do so is to reimagine storage by putting often-used items on rolling carts, leveraging in-between spaces, and having a regular process for getting rid of unneeded items. This has become increasingly important as many people transition to working from home and need their spaces to be even more multifunctional.

Blending areas for leisure and rest with the need for productivity and focus adds another layer of complexity to managing order and tidiness at home. If you're working from home even part of the time, you might be facing these challenges weekly. In this section, I'll focus on managing the complexity of multitasking at home and suggest specific tips for setting up a productive yet stress-free environment.

Putting Your Desk's Prime Real Estate to Use

Let's start with your desk, which for most people is the primary work space. Scan the top of your desk. What's taking up the most space? Chances are most of your desk currently serves as horizontal storage for stacks of paper, miscellaneous documents, pens, and other knickknacks. No matter how necessary these items are, storage is not the main purpose of a desktop. Your goal is to devote the prime real estate on your desk to creative work.

The first step to creating a desktop that allows you to embrace experimentation is to clear it of everything, including your computer, keyboard, lamp, photo frames, everything. Next, use painter's tape to put a vertical and a horizontal strip across the middle of your desk, so it is divided into four equal parts.

Now sort everything into three piles:

1. Items you use every day in your work, such as your pens, computer, and reading glasses. These can go back on your desk into one of the quadrants.

2. Items you've used in the last month. These can go into the desk drawer or rolling storage.

3. Everything else. Discard them or store them elsewhere.

After completing this exercise, rearrange the items from quadrant 1 on your desk however you like. When you're done, 75 percent of your desk should be available for you to adapt according to the work at hand, rather than being used as storage.

Use transparent plastic boxes for storage—
for easy access and to keep things visible.
Stored tools and items will be more readily
available if you're aware and reminded of
their existence. Home goods stores, like
IKEA, sell a great variety of stackable,
visually appealing, and transparent and
semitransparent plastic storage boxes
and units.

Get Out from Behind Your Desk

I encourage you to get up from your chair and out from behind the desk not only as a break from work but also while doing work. Your creative space does not have to be solely done at your desk. Horizontal space attracts clutter. Keep desk objects to a minimum and only for active work. Use shelves or adjacent storage for piles and clutter. Free up space for creativity by taking advantage of your vertical space.

One thing that's almost always underused is wall space, which you probably think of as a place for displaying things. But I encourage you to consider walls as a place for working as well. Carla Diana, a product engineer, uses wall space (not a desk) as a work surface. She designates a wall in her dining room for making sketches of products in various stages of development. Similarly, Rachel Vail, a children's book author, uses the blank wall outside her bathroom as a storyboard. Once you see your walls as work areas, the possibilities are endless.

Up, Up, and Away

I bet you spend a lot of time working at one level—the level of the chair at your desk. But research has found that different heights are better suited for different kinds of work:

STAND (when using a vertical surface for work): Good for brainstorming, being generative, going for quantity of ideas, visual display, showcasing progress.

LEAN IN (when sitting in high barstools at counters or high tables): Good for collaborating, discussing a project, looking at materials together, decision-making.

SIT (when sitting in a medium-high chair at a horizontal surface or table): Good for focusing on solo tasks, making, and executing.

SQUAT (when sitting on low foam cubes, poufs, ottomans, or the floor): Good for listening, observing, talking (twenty-five minutes max for optimal comfort).

Next time you feel stuck, stand up and think through your problem. Write ideas, or sketch or draw them, on colorful sticky notes, along with a few to-dos. Put the notes on the walls, not your desk. Designers call this *space saturation*.

Another easy way to experiment is to sit on the floor or on an ottoman in your office. You can also buy a few inexpensive stackable chairs of varying heights to try out different perspectives (*stackable* is key here for efficient use of space).

DESIGN TIP

Poufs—simple cushioned seats—are attractive and functional design elements that make it easy to transform a room. You can use them for seating and as space dividers, and you can stack them up and store them in the corner when you're done or use them as footrests. Be mindful of color combinations; it's always safe to go with gray (dark or light). Retail and home furniture stores, like Urban Outfitters, sell some affordable ones. Start with five to seven small poufs, or large pillows if using them in the home office. They can also be used in kids' rooms. They're a great investment that will instantly transform your space.

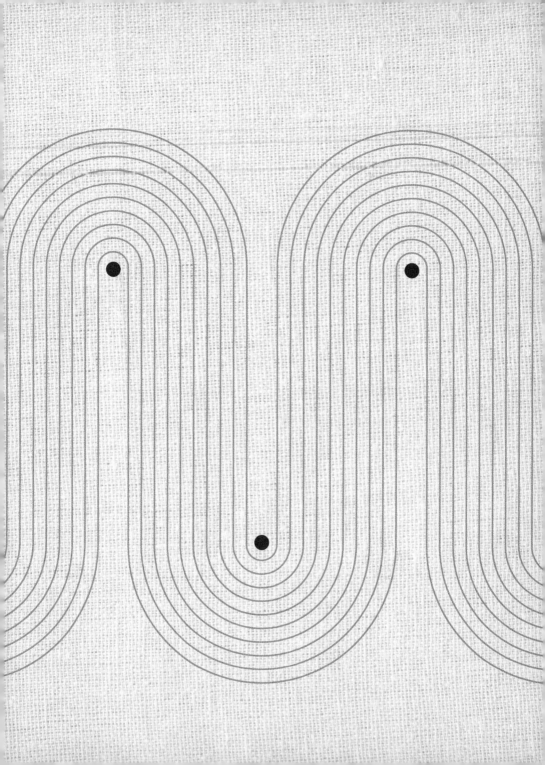

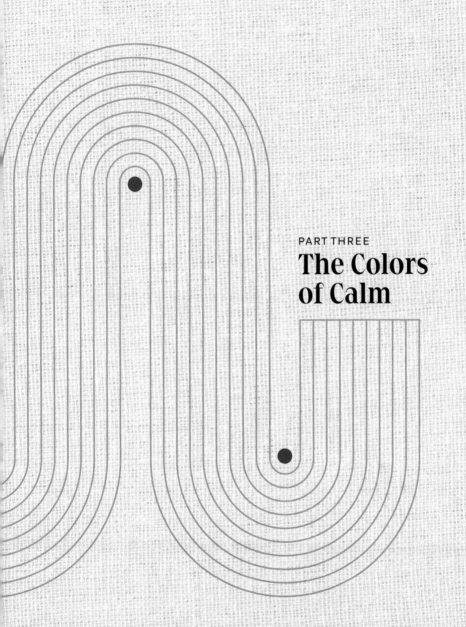

PART THREE

The Colors
of Calm

MOOD
PALETTE

Have you noticed that "How are you doing?" is used as a greeting instead of a question we expect an answer to? This common courtesy that we use to greet strangers and coworkers is not one that we necessarily want answered. This is because, while the question may be simple, the answer often is not. It is hard to put feelings into words on short notice and find a quick answer to such a question.

Last year, I was working with a wonderful designer, Kay, on creating a new mobile app. As part of that project, we collaborated on creating an interactive workshop with multiple key stakeholders. Kay was in charge of the agenda and setup; I was in charge of research and facilitation. This was the first time we'd worked together and, of course, when we met in person, I asked her how she was doing. She replied, "Great."

We met daily for about a week and everything was going well, but Kay had to step out of our planning sessions every hour or so. Toward the end of the week, I noticed how sad Kay looked despite how well the project was going. I asked her again how she was doing, and she broke down. Her father had passed away two weeks before. Her mom lived in Toronto, and Kay had to step out occasionally to call and comfort her mother. I gave her a big hug and some words of consolation. At that point, I wish I had found a better way to understand what she was going through earlier, when I first noticed her sadness.

According to most prominent researchers on emotions, there are at least five universal emotions—fear, anger, sadness, disgust, and enjoyment—each with its own characteristics. For example, sadness is triggered by a feeling of loss, and contains both disappointment and despair. The intensity varies: We can feel mild or strong disappointment. As we worked together, Kay experienced various states of sadness throughout the day, triggered by the loss of her father.

77

Dr. Paul Ekman and his daughter, Dr. Eve Ekman, supported by the Dalai Lama, developed the Atlas of Emotions to help us become more aware of our feelings and more mindful as we move through our days and lives. (Fun fact: This work served as the basis for the Pixar movie *Inside Out*.) According to the Ekmans, each emotion is triggered and then followed by a response.

Practicing mindfulness can help us get in touch with what triggers certain emotions and come up with strategies for responding appropriately. It is not easy to do on the spot. So answering the question "How are you?" is not so simple after all, since it requires first deeply understanding our emotions (with their various states of feelings and triggers) in the moment.

Telegraphing Feelings with Colors

Designers found a way to answer "How are you?" elegantly and effectively though the use of colors. At the beginning of the day, I ask people to pick a color that represents their current mood and share why they picked it, if they're willing to voice such details. It's always surprising how quickly everyone picks a color and how open they are to sharing the reason behind the choice. I wish I had used a quick check-in tool like this with my colleague, Kay, at the beginning of the project to give her an easier way to express what was happening in her life.

The color of the day can help identify emotional hot spots and set the right tone. We often begin our day by making or reviewing to-do lists and tasks. That experience can be anxiety-inducing, setting the wrong tone for the day. What if, instead, you asked yourself about how you're feeling using colors? Walk around your space and place stickies of different colors (representing your feelings) on walls in rooms that trigger emotional hot spots, or even pieces of furniture (e.g., sofa, chair, or kitchen table).

Start the day by getting in touch with how you're feeling using simple colors. Referencing Pantone's wide range of colors can help you represent a greater range of emotions. Here are a few examples of Pantone colors associated with specific feelings: Living Coral or Radiant Orchid (enjoyment), Chili Pepper (fear), Classic Blue (sadness), and Very Peri (a warming, bold lavender tone that represents personal inventiveness and creativity). Develop your own palette of colors based on what colors resonate with your most common feelings. By beginning each morning with a color check-in, you'll have a clearer understanding of how you're feeling and how that might impact your day.

Once you've discovered what colors make you feel most calm and relaxed, consider how you might incorporate them into your space. For example, if mustard yellows make you feel calm, you might add a mustard throw to your couch or a small mustard vase to your workspace.

If You're a Numbers Person

While I was working with the team at Starbucks on new, innovative products, I made a morning ritual of practicing a psychological safety exercise each day. I used a simple two-by-two grid with mood on the vertical axis and energy on the horizontal axis, displaying numbers from 1 to 4. The number 1 represents high energy, high mood, 2 represents high energy, low mood, 3 represents low energy, low mood, and 4 represents low energy, high mood. You can use this as a self-check tool by drawing this grid each morning and then spending a few minutes considering which square you're in. For example, you might self-identify as a 3 if you didn't sleep well last night and are feeling irritable, or a 1 if you're ready to go and full of positive energy.

ENERGY

MOOD

1 = HIGH ENERGY, HIGH MOOD   **3** = LOW ENERGY, LOW MOOD

2 = HIGH ENERGY, LOW MOOD   **4** = LOW ENERGY, HIGH MOOD

Mood-O-Meter

You can use the mood and energy axis to help you better understand how different spaces make you feel. Apply this technique by walking around a room and labeling different areas and objects with a number from 1 to 4, based on how they impact your mood and energy levels. It's rare to always be at a 1, and it is healthy to know whether you're not feeling 100 percent present in a particular area of your dwelling so you can begin to change it (see Setting the Right Intentions for Your Space, page 39). Alternatively, you can draw the mood and energy axis on a large poster, and then write down names of furniture or areas of your home on sticky notes. Plot the sticky notes on the grid to spotlight what areas drain you and what areas uplift you.

Expressing your feelings with colors should go beyond creating a mood board and can be translated to furniture and your general surroundings. I would encourage you to adopt natural fabrics and materials with light, soft colors—those that are often associated with the Japandi style, a blend of Japanese and Scandinavian design—to give your brain a rest. Replacing heaviness with light in your palette (both the one that you use to express your emotions and the one you surround yourself with in your home) will promote tranquility, keeping you more centered and focused on what matters most, instead of being distracted by a variety of colors that don't represent your mood and well-being (see Replace Heaviness with Light, page 102).

FOCUSED
SATURATION

You've probably seen the iconic Eames Lounge
Chair when you shopped or browsed for
furniture. Created by a couple of American
industrial designers, Charles and Ray Eames, in
the late 1950s, it became a hallmark of modern
design, versatility, and uniqueness. Charles and
Ray were a married couple who made significant contributions to the field of design in
the twentieth century; collaborated with each
other on architecture, furniture, and graphic
design projects, as well as fine art and film; and
inspired generations of designers. They established the Eames House—the couple's home
and creative hub where creatives gathered in an
informal setting—as well as the Eames Office,
a design studio where innovative products were
developed. When I studied their work in school,
I often wondered how Charles and Ray were
able to sustain their creativity, productivity, and
marriage over the course of four decades.

An insight into this came later when I met Marinus and Kim Vandenberg, a present-day version of the Eameses. The Vandenbergs are another design power couple who specialize in branding and marketing of products in the food and beverage and health and wellness industries. I was instantly enamored with their intellectual curiosity, worldliness, and hospitality. They welcomed me into their home in Berkeley, California, for dinner and showed me their design studio, which was housed downstairs. Unlike the Eameses' setup, house and office were in the same location but with a clear delineation.

Stepping into their office, I got the same feeling as when I first set foot in Stanford's d.school. The studio space was saturated with visuals: mood boards, brainstorming stickies, branding ideas, project time lines, photography—most at eye level. Marinus and Kim had their desks facing each other, with large computer monitors sitting on top, but their work wasn't confined to their computers. It was all around them in a focused saturation, prompting discussion, idea flow, and creativity. I was so inspired that I have since tried to replicate this setup for myself and encourage you to do the same, or at least to borrow certain elements that may work for you.

Inspire at Eye Level

Your space offers a vast opportunity to inspire and aspire. Don't waste the opportunity of sparking inspiration with empty spaces. Surrounding yourself with images, charts, and notes can provoke creative thinking and action. You can begin by adding images to a Pinterest page, but ultimately you should transfer images to a bulletin board, foam board, tri-fold display, or walls—something that will catch your eye during the day. Think vertical, not just horizontal, and beyond your desk; wrap your space with inspiration.

Your brain links concepts that are unspoken and unseen. Think of your immediate surroundings as a teleprompter sending stimulus to your brain. Regularly changing what you see around your area (so you're not staring at the same thing all the time) allows your brain to connect ideas, actions, and people in unexpected ways.

DESIGN TIP

Mood boards are a great way to stimulate thinking. To add a mood board to your space, use a bulletin board or a large foam core board (black works best; you can also use a tri-fold display board) and set it up on or against a wall where you can continuously add visuals to prompt new ideas and get re-inspired.

Mood boards can be used for any project or subject matter. For example, if you're a novelist, you might put together a mood board about the characters or locations you're writing about.

Surrounding yourself with images and information will stimulate your thinking. If a visual in a magazine catches your eye, tear it out and hang it on your mood board, even if you don't immediately know why it intrigues you. If you see an interesting statistic or headline, type it out in bold type and print a copy for your mood board so that you can ponder the information. The mood board is an easy and quick way to instantly transform your space into an area for inspiration.

Your Head Needs Headspace

Given a choice of rooms to engage in creativity, here's a tip: Pick the one with the higher ceiling. Extra headroom encourages freer, more abstract thinking. When researchers divided participants into two rooms, one with a ten-foot ceiling and another where they deliberately lowered the height to eight feet, they found the group in the room with the higher ceiling were more likely to say they felt free, creative, unlimited, and unbound than those in the lower-ceilinged space. The researchers concluded creativity flows when you have not only adequate mental space but also physical space.

While it's unlikely you have the ability to raise the ceiling of your space, it is possible to trick your brain into the illusion of space and perspective. When I walk into a windowed room, I have to fight the urge to turn all the desks to face the window. Desks oriented toward the wall are suitable for a room supporting concentration and individual work, but spaces that support brainstorming should have an outward focus. Orient your desk, if possible, to allow your eye to look outside a window. If your outside view is a brick wall, the benefits diminish, but you'd be surprised by what a little natural light and vista can do to open up your perspective and creativity.

If a view of the outdoors is not in the cards, you still can lighten up any room easily and inexpensively using a designer's secret weapon—mirrors. Try placing a mirror where it catches and reflects natural light back to you.

Another way to create perspective is to hang art in your line of sight. When you see a piece of art you love, the flow of blood increases to the brain. Some offices invest in expensive original works, but posters of paintings have the same effect. Just choose images you love and rotate them.

If you find yourself staring at a computer screen all day, change your screen saver option to display a variety of images. The Art Institute of Chicago is the latest museum to make its collection available for download. Take advantage of digitized art in the public domain to expose yourself to a variety of art via your computer screen to stimulate your brain.

Walls Let You Concentrate

While high ceilings encourage creative thinking, when you need to concentrate, think of the opposite. Low ceilings don't let the mind wander, which is beneficial when you need to focus. Similarly, walls close the mind to distractions; they aid memory and concentration. Therefore, the key to rooms effective for focus is walls. Lots of them. Walls allow you to focus and contain your thinking to the problem at hand and help your brain process and track many moving parts.

When it comes to the work environment, the amount of distraction in an open-plan office can make it a challenge to focus. Some offices have installed phone booths or pods in the middle of a big open space and if you have access to such solitary spaces, take advantage of them. However, there usually aren't enough of them. How, then, do you construct a pocket of privacy in an open space?

Here are some ways to create de facto walls: Use a bookshelf to create a barrier between you and others. Relocate a whiteboard to the edge of your space. (You don't actually have to use it.) Surround your desk with potted plants. Bring in a coat hanger and coat for a curtained effect. Another option is to create a virtual wall. Noise-canceling technology isn't just for listening to music. Use headphones to develop a sound barrier between you and everyone else. Or use freestanding devices that generate white noise or dampen outside sounds to give you peace and quiet.

Create a Visual Reflection of Progress

When you plaster a room with notes, you take advantage of spatial memory. Knowing where the information is increases your ability to remember what the content is. That's why whiteboards, oversize papers, and sticky notes help you organize information.

And when you capture every decision and put it on the wall, you don't have to worry whether everyone is on the same page. The room is the page. The more you put on the walls, the more shared understanding you build. As a bonus, you spend less time revisiting already-discussed issues. A dedicated room works great for projects lasting days or a few weeks. It also works great for one-off meetings.

Remember the oversize thermometer in the background of televised pledge drives with the red line rising with each new donation?

The image allowed viewers at home to follow the influx of donations, an activity that occurs off camera through phone calls or online.

We are visual animals. As a reminder of the goal to be met, the thermometer creates a visual challenge that helps viewers solve the problem—namely, raising money for the cause. As the thermometer goes higher and higher, we feel a sense of accomplishment. Along with that sense of accomplishment comes a sense of community. We're in it together! Watching a fundraising thermometer's progress lets donors know that others are involved with the fundraising too. That social proof is a compelling reason to get involved and can inspire otherwise undecided donors to engage. It is why including suggested donation amounts on a donation form inspires larger gifts: We want to give the way our peers give, and seeing our peers give makes us want to be involved. All this with one simple visual.

The same dynamic happens at any sporting event where the scoreboard not only keeps track of each team's standing but also serves as a prompt for how the crowd should react. Anyone from players and coaches to referees and fans can see in an instant their team's standing by glancing at the scoreboard.

We humans love to see and track progress. Short of a thermometer or scoreboard, how can you create the same sense of progress and community in your setting? You can make use of inexpensive and common materials such as posters, bulletin boards, empty walls, or other visuals in the work space to remind yourself and team members of the goal and the progress made toward the goal. Even a small space can be used for showing off your progress. Adding a sticky note to your desk with yesterday's wins or setting your screen saver to reflect last month's sales figures are small-space ways to remind yourself of what you've accomplished.

DESIGN TIP

Celebrating your joy is a lovely way to help cultivate peace and calm. A simple way to do this is to showcase and celebrate moments of your life in a mini "pop-up" gallery. You can use a whiteboard, the wall, shelves, or a portion of your desk as your gallery space and fill the space with uplifting mementos. For example, you can print out photos taken on your phone during a recent trip, frame sketches or doodles that make you smile, tape up journaling pages with positive words or affirmations, or position small gifts from someone special on a shelf in your workspace. Refresh your gallery each month. Being surrounded by these reminders of joy can bring instant calm during a hectic day.

Saturate Your Space

Your space should allow you to capture and display ideas (or even doodles) as they arise, since conversations and ideas don't always conveniently happen at a desk or near the computer. You should have sticky notes and markers readily available to capture ideas where they strike. If you're not sure what ideas to capture, or even what inspiring images to print and display, I'd suggest doing and displaying "meaningless" work first. A drawing class often starts with simple sketching; track practice begins with a warm-up. Likewise, your day can start with your version of doodles or warm-ups to prepare your brain and body for the coming day.

Visually surrounding yourself with inspiring images, organizing them into mood boards or collages, choosing themes to explore, and visually saturating and grouping ideas can provoke creative thinking and doing. Showcasing work, projects, or aspirations can help visually celebrate this work and progress. Signage, displays, even storage become an important representation of elevating your work. This brings to the surface your creative process—your way of thinking and doing.

Through focused saturation, you can activate your space, encouraging creative practices and rituals (see Setting the Right Intentions for Your Space, page 39). Communicating work in an impactful and meaningful way by using illustrative visuals is one of the tools that designers use most effectively. But anyone—designers and non-designers alike—can visually represent their work, project progress, and creative process in a physical environment.

REPLACE HEAVINESS WITH LIGHT

A few years ago, a close friend and fellow designer, Rachel, was going through a difficult divorce. The experience was both devastating and liberating for her—devastating because Rachel had a young daughter with her ex-husband and liberating because their relationship was over due to unforeseen, complicated circumstances.

Shortly after the divorce, Rachel took her daughter on a trip to Oahu—a serene Hawaiian island—to calm down and reset during a mother-daughter vacation. She was in awe of the island's beauty, the welcoming and kind aloha spirit, and the Asian design influences in her accommodations. When Rachel came back from her summer trip, she reached out to me to help her figure out a way to re-create this at home. She wanted to both physically and emotionally replace heaviness with light.

Simple changes to our space can offset the emotional weight of anxiety, sadness, and stress. For example, clean air, proportionality (e.g., furniture that's lower to the ground) and the clutter-to-empty space ratio (e.g., keep shelves half empty) have a tremendous effect, giving us breathing room. We can create more breathing room by borrowing a few concepts from the Japandi design style.

This style was created by combining Scandinavian minimalist design principles, to create comfort with the right amount of items, with the philosophy of wabi-sabi, finding beauty in the imperfect, which comes from Japanese design. To achieve the serenity that Rachel found in Oahu and was looking to replicate in her own space, I recommended a few practical tips on applying Japandi at home.

Go Down to Earth

To begin with, lower the height of furniture in your room. For instance, by lowering the bed in your bedroom, the ease of its use increases because you're closer to the ground. You literally feel more grounded—more stable, at ease, and consciously present—in your existence. In Rachel's case, we replaced her old bed with a low-profile tatami bed—a Japanese platform bed consisting of a solid wood frame and a futon mattress.

Alternatively, you can acquire furniture with taller legs that you can see underneath to visually create more space for your eyes (e.g., armchairs with taller legs that are not too heavy and dark). This is especially applicable to smaller spaces, like apartments or living rooms, which are not too spacious. This lifting of furniture off the ground instantly creates an airier look, even if you can't physically increase the square footage of your space.

In my friend's living room, two heavy, square, brown leather armchairs were weighing down the entire living room and taking up too much space. As you walked in, your eyes instantly gravitated toward them and you felt too anchored, almost buried. We ended up putting her old armchairs up for sale on one of the online marketplaces and found two light-gray, midcentury ones as replacements, which instantly gave Rachel's living room more space and definition.

Use Light and Functional Materials

Following minimalist and clean lines along with using light and functional materials is another characteristic of this style. But you don't have to replace everything at once. In Rachel's case, we started small by focusing on fabrics and replacing bedding, place mats, and kitchen towels with light, natural cotton or linen ones. When you walk into her bedroom or kitchen now, you immediately notice the difference and feel lighter. As you look around the room, these natural fabrics seamlessly blend and don't strain your eyes.

The next thing we focused on was tableware since she used this daily and visually experienced it all the time, and it's relatively inexpensive to switch out. We landed on

Japanese porcelain pottery called Hasami (for more detail on Hasami, see Keep Comfort Within Reach, page 55). These clean, simple, and functional plates, mugs, and bowls look both modern yet traditional, are easily stackable, serve multiple purposes, and conserve space.

Create Decluttered Spaces

In Japandi style, every piece has a purpose. Periodically doing a bit of an inventory helps identify which items have lost their purpose and which have gained multipurpose functionality. A great way to do this is by conducting an assessment of your space and various items in it (see Energy Inventory, page 145) to determine what to keep or toss. If you follow minimalist and clean lines, then you eventually declutter spaces, which is another characteristic of this style.

Dr. Andrew Huberman, a Stanford neurobiologist and ophthalmologist, has conducted research on a visual mode that can change our stress levels and make us calmer. He describes *panoramic vision*, or optic flow, as the following: "When [you] look at a horizon or at a broad vista, you don't look at one thing for very long. If you keep your head still, you can dilate your gaze so you can see far into the periphery—above, below, and to the sides of you. That mode of vision releases a mechanism in the brain stem involved in vigilance and arousal. We can actually turn off the stress response by changing the way that we are viewing our environment, regardless of what's in that environment."

Although we can't necessarily create the same panoramic view you get when you're in nature looking at the sunset on a beach, you can achieve a similar result by creating decluttered spaces and practicing a simple exercise of lowering your gaze, defocusing, and slowly scanning the room from left to right and back, while being intentional with your breath. This will help you be calm, centered, and present.

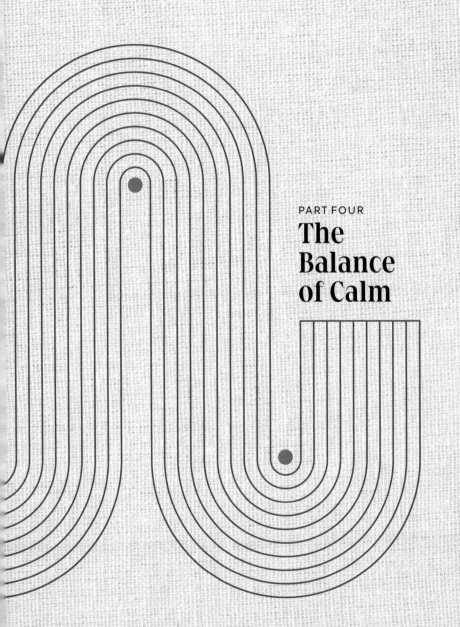

PART FOUR

The Balance of Calm

BRING THE OUTSIDE IN

The natural world offers us endless inspiration for calm design. One phenomenal example of nature influencing design can be seen at the Sea Ranch, a group of houses that was built along the Pacific coast in California's Sonoma County in the 1960s. Joseph Esherick and George Homsey were two of several prominent architects to contribute to a hybrid of modern and vernacular architecture in the Sea Ranch community. At the Sea Ranch, "the buildings become part of the landscape, not subordinate to it, but do not dominate either. Details such as exteriors of unpainted wood or muted stains, a lack of overhanging eaves, and baffles on exterior lighting subdue the appearance of the buildings in the landscape. . . . The lack of roof overhangs is also intended to allow the near-constant strong breezes to pass over the buildings without the turbulence the overhangs would create." As you walk by the buildings at night, you'll notice the effects of minimal lighting along with the lack of streetlights that allow you to fully enjoy the night sky. The Sea Ranch is a fantastic example of architecture working together with nature and the "outside-in" approach of bringing elements of nature indoors.

This approach greatly influenced some work I did recently, when my team and I were asked to facilitate an off-site for Esherick Homsey Dodge and Davis (EHDD), one of the top architecture firms in the San Francisco Bay Area. They were about to kick off a major project with tight deadlines and anticipated high levels of stress. The leadership team had asked us to spark creativity and imagination while building on the legacy of EHDD projects, such as the Sea Ranch.

We drew inspiration for the workshop from the Esalen Institute, another example of the outside-in approach, again from the California of the '60s and '70s. By some accounts, several well-known creativity programs in the Bay Area can be traced back to personal awareness work and alternative workshops developed at Esalen—an iconic Northern California education center founded in the 1960s during the Human Potential Movement.

The Esalen retreat and spa center is situated above the rugged oceanside bluffs of Big Sur. The property sits on twenty-seven beautiful acres, and the site's cliff-hugging soaking tubs are heated by natural hot springs. Educators at Esalen focus on the mind-body connection: expressing feelings through sound (voice) without meaning (i.e., words), thinking through movement, and using color and the drawing or painting of non-objects as ways to express thoughts and feelings. They would often challenge assumptions and rely on tactile sensations for exploration or decision-making.

The first thing we had the workshop participants do was sit on the floor and silently count rice grains; this was followed by a debrief about how that made them feel. We deliberately chose counting rice as a low-energy warm-up activity that served as a precursor to the following activity, which was more intense. We cleared the room of all furniture and gave everyone blank sheets of paper and a small pile of rice grains.

Workshop facilitators didn't explicitly state that everyone had to remain in the crowded room to count—we actually wanted to see how creative folks would get with completing the exercise. We were hoping they would "bring the outside in," as the Sea Ranch or Esalen do. But to our dismay, most people kneeled or sat on the floor as they counted their rice while only a few pulled up chairs from the lobby or left the room entirely to go back to their cubicles or a more comfortable setting like the waiting room with a view of the bay. After about ten minutes, they were done counting the rice—grouping by twos or tens, for example, or circling piles of five.

During the debrief, we asked how many rice grains each person counted—one hundred each! Then we asked what participants thought the point of the exercise was. Some said it was to get to the right number, while others thought it was to count as quickly or as effectively as possible. But we never deliberately stated that in our instructions: the goal was simply to count the rice grains! Next, we asked why some people remained in uncomfortable positions while counting, why they didn't consider leaving the room or bringing more comfortable furniture in, and why they didn't give themselves permission to change their environment. Once again, we never explicitly forbade the architects from leaving the space or grabbing some furniture from another conference room, so that limitation was entirely self-imposed.

Although slowing down and counting the rice helped the architects stay focused and calm amid their hectic projects, it also created space for self-inquiry and challenged their assumptions about space constraints. The point of the exercise was to highlight how we often self-constrain and limit our imaginations. With the original Sea Ranch design, the architects were breaking ground by leveraging elements they found outside the building, using out-of-the-box thinking and challenging traditional assumptions. We needed to get back to that place of creativity and out-of-the-box thinking again for their next project, and this was the first step.

This focused rice-counting activity not only helps create calm but also serves as a reminder to be intentional about your space and conscious of simple choices that can have a bigger impact on your life than you realize. Consider what unnecessary limitations you're placing on yourself and the ways you undertake tasks within a given space. What might you try differently today?

A simple way to bring the outdoors in is to fill your space with plants. I recommend choosing a variety of low-maintenance plants—snake plant, Monstera, ficus, bird-of-paradise, fiddle-leaf fig tree, succulents—and mixing and matching tall and short plants strikes a nice aesthetic balance. I'm a big fan of tiny habits, or small steps toward a bigger goal (see Setting the Right Intentions for Your Space, page 39), and adding plants to your space is a small step that can lead to other calming design choices. Filling your space with greenery not only literally brings the outdoors in but also inspires at eye level and prompts you to incorporate other nature-inspired colors, textures, and materials into your space later, as you bring in new furniture pieces, bedding, or tableware.

FLARING
AND
FOCUSING

When artist Anna Gaskell moved her expanding family to a duplex in New York City, she hadn't planned on working from home. "My husband and I would say goodbye, and both leave for the office every morning. Even though my work isn't a traditional job, I needed to *go* to work," Anna told me.

Since arriving in New York in 1996, fresh from earning her MFA from Yale University, Anna earned praise and comparisons to Cindy Sherman. Her first solo show sold out before the opening and the Guggenheim and the Museum of Modern Art (MoMA) acquired her works. She'd always maintained a studio close to home. Still, one day after dashing back for yet another toddler emergency, Anna knew she needed to make a work space in her home.

Her duplex featured a wide central space that served multiple purposes: entertaining, dining, play, and now Anna's work. The challenge was to accommodate a teenager and his friends, an active toddler, the babysitter, and visitors—while still pushing the creative envelope.

Embracing experimentation requires being open to new ideas. Even if your inspirational space is just a corner of your home, it should still invite you to see and try new things. That point was underscored for Anna when Svetlana Lunkina, a former prima ballerina of the Bolshoi Ballet, came over for coffee after they met at a gallery opening.

"As I poured her espresso, I noticed every movement she made, even turning her head to thank me, conveyed this incredible muscle control. I thought, *Wouldn't it be cool to capture that raw power in portraits.*" Anna asked Svetlana if she could take a few test shots, and because her home had open space, Svetlana demonstrated a few dance moves, which laid the groundwork for a more formal session later. The resulting portraits were shown at galleries and toured all over Europe.

Anna's impromptu photo shoot with Svetlana involved what we call *flaring*, the process of divergent thinking where you're open to ideas and inspirations. Transforming her living room into a mini dance studio by pushing furniture against the wall allowed Anna to explore a passing idea that might otherwise have been lost in the moment.

Creativity, which often comes after calm and clarity, requires both divergent thinking and convergent thinking, two distinct modes that require different behaviors—and space requirements. When I hear coworkers say, "I'm flaring," I know they are in experimental mode. They're brainstorming and open to ideas. Someone who is flaring may seek a large number of inputs because the goal isn't to find the single best idea as much as to stay open to wide possibilities, no matter how far-fetched. Meanwhile, if a colleague says, "I'm focusing," they have already winnowed the set of possibilities to specific solutions and are looking for critical input. At this point, they don't need more ideas but rather to assess the viability of the ones at hand. If I had held back concerns during the flaring stage, now would be the time to offer constructive criticism.

DESIGN TIP

FLARING calls for divergent thinking, whereby you look for the *most* solutions to a problem.

FOCUSING requires convergent thinking, with the goal of finding *one* idea or a small subset of ideas that are worth further investment of time and resources to develop.

Even when you're working by yourself, you still must determine whether you're flaring or focusing. Once you identify whether you're in a generative or an evaluative mode, the next step is to distinguish the behaviors—and space requirements— needed to support the underlying work. Consider what objects, furniture, lighting, sounds, and rituals support you when you're in flaring mode versus focusing mode.

A Place for Flaring

Flaring requires stimulation. How can you identify the best locations for opening your mind to ideas?

BRING IN THE LIGHT: When I see a desk facing a wall, I wonder how much of the person's work involves flaring. While this setup would be suitable for focusing activities, it is not as conducive to opening you up to new ideas. If possible, choose a work area facing outward. A window is best. If your window faces a brick wall, obviously the benefits diminish, but research shows natural light and even a little piece of sky can open up your imagination.

CHANGE YOUR VIEW: Don't worry if you lack an open area for flaring. The trick is to break the fixed patterns your brain loves so much and force it to rethink the world. You can accomplish this by working in another part of your house or office—the kitchen counter, living room, or conference room, for example. It's okay if the area is noisy.

I recommend placing items you use occasionally on rolling carts with wheels to move them around more easily and make your space more flexible. Having storage in corners or against the wall creates wasted space that could be used for creativity.

Changing your perspective can do wonders for your imagination. When everything is exactly as you expect, your brain falls back into its usual habits. If your day feels stale or unproductive, take a minute to identify what environmental factors are present. Sometimes simply changing one or two elements, such as your seating arrangement, can transform the entire tone of the day. If all else fails, walk your dog (or yourself) for a guaranteed brain and heart boost.

A Place for Focusing

Let's turn to spaces for focusing. Once you've amassed a bunch of ideas, you have to identify the ones that are worth pursuing. This requires in-depth research, number crunching, and the painful task of taking ideas off the list. You have to get systematic, critical, and ruthless when evaluating options.

In contrast to flaring, the vibe here is on narrowing, not brainstorming or creative meandering. The focusing mentality is one of thoroughness and critical thinking. You're trying to drive projects to completion. How can your space support this work?

BARRICADE YOURSELF: The answer is low ceilings and walls. Walls allow you to focus and contain your thinking to the problem at hand; they aid memory and concentration. Not only that, but a room with barriers also helps the brain process and track lots of moving parts.

You likely can't move the ceilings and walls in your home, but you can create de facto walls that close you inside your work space. Remember Anna's open room? She evaluated the portraits she took of Svetlana and refined her ideas at a desk she keeps at the back of her duplex behind a wall of books. Potted plants can have the same effect. If a vertical barrier doesn't work, try delineating your work space with a handsome rug. Your goal is to keep your brain contained and focused on the work at hand.

TRACK YOUR PROGRESS: Focusing is about moving toward a goal. One way to track progress is by taking advantage of spatial memory. Knowing *where* the information is increases your ability to remember *what* the information is. That's why keeping track of your progress visually in your space can help you organize your work. Posters with project time lines and milestones are one example of this (see Focused Saturation, page 86, for more ideas).

Creating visual representations of our workflow and accomplishments can help us feel more calm and grounded. A great way to do this is through creating a kanban board, a visual tool that makes it easy to track progress over time. A basic kanban board can be made using sticky notes on a whiteboard to show progress. Divide a board into columns that represent stages of the work. With stickies representing key goals, events, or activities, you can move the notes from left to right to record project movement and coordinate efforts with others.

If you're in tight quarters, try finding small ways to capture and visualize your work accomplishments and goals. Tacking a sticky note on your computer with yesterday's sales figures or setting your screen saver with this month's big action items are small-space ways to remind yourself of what you've accomplished and make progress toward your goal.

Flaring and Focusing in the Same Space

Most of us don't have the luxury of keeping separate spaces for flaring and focusing. We do both kinds of work in the same space (i.e., your desk). Because you usually go through flaring and focusing stages multiple times throughout a project, your space should support you in these creative but opposing moments. The key is to establish ways to reset your space and brain.

If you need to engage in flaring and focusing in short order, break up the activities by doing each separately and at least taking a pause between the sessions. Stand up, move around, and clear your mind before the next phase.

RESETTING: To reset yourself, try turning your desk (if possible) to suit the mode you're in. Turn it to face outward if you're in flaring mode and toward the wall when you're in focusing mode. The same idea can be accomplished with L-shaped desks or where there is room on two sides to work. Move your chair from one side of the desk to the other to change your orientation.

REMIND YOURSELF: Resetting can be as easy as displaying signs with either "flaring" or "focusing" imprinted on them as a visual reminder of the current mode you're in. This seems simple but it works. At your desk, display one or the other sign. If you work with others, it will signal whether you are avoiding distraction or welcoming collaboration. You can also set a status on your computer to indicate this for virtual work.

BE INTENTIONAL: Flaring and focusing are distinct and critical states. Regardless of whether you're in a large room with multiple participants or alone at your desk, understanding which mode you're in and how the environment can support you will give you greater clarity about how to achieve your goal.

BEING
ALONE
TOGETHER

Have you ever wondered how coffee shops create ambient environments for working together—alone? How you arrange furniture and objects greatly influences how you act in that space: placing sofas and chairs across from each other to encourage face-to-face communication, having a convenient place to set drinks while you relax. The right placement makes your life easier and less stressful; so does matching noise to mood. Quick space experiments, such as pop-ups for collaborating, creative space combinations for working alone, or multipurpose mash-ups can help balance being alone together.

Svetlana Royzen, a talented baker and the owner of Light Confection in San Francisco, got her start baking meringues. Svetlana experimented with unusual ingredients to elevate this simple treat, traditionally made with egg whites, sugar, and flour, by adding rose water or chili powder to the mix, dipping the bottoms in dark chocolate, and decorating with dried edible flowers, mulberries, or crushed pistachio nuts. She wasn't sure whether there was ever going to be a market for her culinary creations, so before taking out a loan from a bank to open up a proper bakery, she sought advice from a few friends in the food and beverage industry.

A wine bar owner in the city suggested Svetlana first do a pop-up inside his bar. They worked out a short tasting menu with meringues of different flavors paired with a few champagnes and white wines. Every month, Svetlana took over a corner of the wine bar and set up a small display, a table with a prix fixe tasting menu for drinks and treats. They promoted the pop-up on social media, and she was able to gauge the interest level of potential customers, gather feedback, and explore this potential partnership in a lightweight yet practical way. This let her take an important step toward her dream before making drastic changes or commitments in her life.

You've probably seen pop-ups like Svetlana's in other coffee shops, in galleries, or even at universities. When I was contemplating teaching a new class on mindfulness and environments with colleagues from design school, we landed on first teaching a pop-up class—an experimental, short-format workshop that would help us prototype and improve what wasn't yet fully formed and articulated. The same concept can be applied at home. You can set up a temporary pop-up in an area of your home to try out a different configuration. For example, once a month you can try re-creating a coffee shop vibe and set up a similar temporary environment by moving pieces of furniture to face each other.

Set Up a Temporary Pop-Up

Even with the right intentions, your space may not serve you as intended. Remember Anna Gaskell, the artist who lives in a duplex in New York City with her family while also working from home (see Flaring and Focusing, page 119)? Anna quickly realized the studio inside her duplex, which was supposed to help her push the creative envelope, instead had turned into a common family area where everyone congregated and left toys, clothes, and food items.

What do you do when your work space, with kids and pets in the mix, gets used as a play-room during the time you feel most creative? Don't despair. Consider making your work space portable. You can make use of different nooks of your home by setting up temporary pop-up spaces for yourself. Take over a specific area for a few days—a corner of your living room, for example—and see what you need to make it work. Get a foldout chair and a small writing surface (or a long bench and a short table). Treat it like a coffee shop—working alone, together—since you most likely won't be the sole inhabitant of that area for long.

Getting out of a fixed setup can get you out of your fixed mindset, boosting creative problem solving. You don't have to think of your space in terms of fixed categories: living room, office, bedroom. Rather, consider the intended use and apply creative combinations that can be multipurpose depending on the situation, people, and context. Even with the right intentions, your space may not serve you as intended.

I Like, I Wish, What If?

Once you've created a temporary pop-up in an area of your home or office and spent some time there, use this I Like, I Wish, What If? practice to evaluate how successful (or not successful) the experiment was. Over time, you'll have a record of what worked best, and you can consider combining those elements into a more permanent solution.

To conduct this evaluation, write an answer in your journal to each of the following prompts:

I like . . . (What you liked about the experiment, note any specific details, and always start with something positive.)

I wish . . . (What you wish were different, in other words, note what didn't work as well or could have been improved.)

What if? (Write down any new ideas for next time, or some elements you'd like to keep as a permanent design solution.)

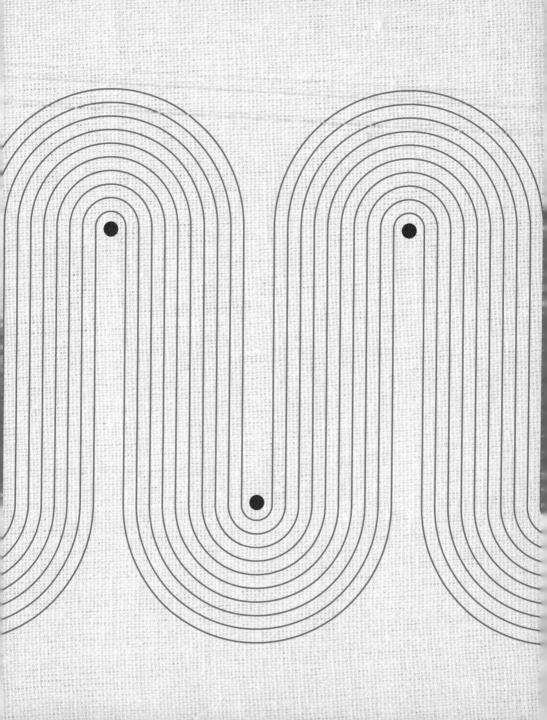

PART FIVE

Centering Your Calm

YOUR CALM-
DOWN
CORNER

A few years ago, I received a phone call in the middle of the night. It was my dear friend Lena, whom I've known for more than a decade; our parents knew each other, and our kids played together. Lena and her husband, Roland, who are avid travelers and certified scuba divers, traveled every year to new destinations, even after they had two rowdy boys.

That year, they went to the beautiful island of Cozumel in the Caribbean Sea to explore the surrounding coral reefs. On the first day of their trip, Roland decided to go for an afternoon swim while Lena and the kids rested in the hotel room after a long journey. The sudden phone call I received from her that night bore tragic news. Roland had unexpectedly passed away.

Lena was devastated, and the tough times that followed came with support from her family, friends, and community. We launched a fundraising campaign, brought meals, and picked up her kids from school. One day when I asked Lena what else we could do for her, she said, "I appreciate all the help, but I need some space to think. What I really want is to clear my house of the clutter so I can sit with my feelings and reset."

While her response wasn't what I expected, it didn't surprise me either. We all crave a little space for ourselves, yet all day long, the rooms we occupy often reflect other people's needs or ad hoc decisions made without a vision of supporting and inspiring our spirit. How do we intentionally carve out space that invites us to breathe and be alone with our thoughts and feelings?

A fantastic role model of such intentionality is Steve Jobs, the founder of Apple. According to Walter Isaacson's biography of Steve Jobs, the tech giant lived most of his life in a sparsely furnished house. In a photograph taken in 1982, you can see Jobs sitting cross-legged on the wooden floor with a cup of tea in a nearly empty room in his house in Woodside, California. For the longest time, according to Isaacson, it contained only a chest of drawers, a mattress, a card table, and some folding chairs for guests. Even when the house filled with his growing family, he and his wife continued to debate furniture selection with great care, asking themselves, "What is the purpose of a sofa? Is this really needed?" This is the perfect example of intentionally creating a design that supports individual needs and giving oneself permission to exist in a space that does not conform to standard expectations.

A Corner of Calm

Based on my work creating intentional environments, I recommended Lena design a *calm-down corner,* repurposing a part of her home she could claim as hers alone, where she didn't feel pressure to cook, clean, work, sleep, socialize, or do anything at all.

A guest room can serve as an ideal resetting space because it is only needed sporadically. The basement or part of the garage may work too. Some people have gone so far as to build a separate meditation room, but that's not necessary. The only requirement is that your calm-down spot is somewhere that promotes peace and tranquility.

With two boys, Lena's home didn't engender a lot of peace and tranquility. As Lena and I walked the inside perimeter of her home, assessing every area, we paid special attention to the corners. Have you noticed how corners tend to be underused? We passed a cluttered nook to the side of the open living room. It was dark and cramped; the energy surrounding it was chaotic because it served as de facto storage for knickknacks. "If the kids don't know where something goes, it ends up there," she said.

"Let's see what we can do with it," I suggested.

Energy Inventory

Are there areas of your home that make you feel uncomfortable or stressed? Or maybe there's a room that makes you involuntarily smile when you walk into it. You may not even be able to place your finger on why, but some areas feel out of balance while others exude peace and tranquility.

Choosing an area that gives you positive energy is critical to creating a space for resetting. To understand how you react to different areas, I recommend you take an energy inventory by moving around your home and noting which areas give you energy and which drain you.

Step 1

> Move through your space with sticky notes and a marker. Notice how you feel in each room, nook, or part of your dwelling.

> Write a plus on a sticky note if a space feels energy-giving or a minus if it is energy-draining. Rely on your initial gut feeling; don't overthink this.

> Assess spaces, furniture, or objects with notes. You can also use different colors to color-code: green or yellow for positive vibes and red or purple for negative.

EXERCISE

Your goal is to pay attention to emotional details and note the unintentional choices you are already making in your home. For example, we all have our favorite place to sit. In our house, it's the office couch, and while I tried to make our living room comfortable and inviting with a grand sofa, everyone in our household, for some reason, still gravitates toward the office.

Step 2

> **Next, brainstorm at least three ways to decrease the drain or increase the energy by writing each idea down on a sticky note and putting it in that area. Use the following Rules of Brainstorming to guide this session:**
>
> > **One Idea at a Time**
> >
> > **Go for Quantity**
> >
> > **Headline!**
> >
> > **Build on Your Ideas**
> >
> > **Encourage Wild Ideas**
> >
> > **Be Visual**
> >
> > **Stay on Topic**
> >
> > **Defer Judgment**

(Optional) Get out of the building! Get inspired before you brainstorm by conducting analogous research in spaces you like to visit and work at outside of your home.

EXERCISE

In your notebook, make a list of the top ten energy-giving activities and identify various environments where those actions or behaviors are typically exhibited. If you feel more creative while writing in a coffee shop, start thinking about what makes that environment conducive to creativity.

Go there and notice what makes that space supportive of the behaviors you want your space to encourage—such as having your favorite beverage, working alone together, or being surrounded by the hustle and bustle of the café.

Take notes in your notebook, or photos and videos on your phone, to fuel your brainstorming. Borrow what works there and make it happen in your own space, even if it's a small change, such as buying a fancy espresso maker.

Step 3

Focus on what matters most by voting for your *low-hanging fruit*, *darling*, and *moon shot*. You can use voting dots to vote for up to three ideas in each category. Put a green dot next to the low-hanging fruit, a red one next to your darling or most likely to delight, and a blue one next to your moon shot. Here are a few personal examples:

147

EXERCISE

Low-Hanging Fruit

- Smile first thing in the morning.
- Stand up every hour.
- Rethink the indoor temperature.

Darling

- Get more succulents for the living room.
- Repaint the walls.

Moon Shot

- Break down walls to create more open space and increase natural light.

In Lena's case, we ended up picking one place as her meditation or reflecting space and removing as many things from it as possible. You should continue to embrace experimentation in your space by periodically reassessing how it makes you feel. By playing around with, or prototyping, different arrangements, you can determine whether you feel better in your space post-redesign and get more energy from being in it.

Resetting to Zero

The cluttered nook in Lena's house had the advantage of not having any sight lines directly into the space. It felt private despite the lack of a door. In addition, other than as a repository for miscellaneous objects, it wasn't being used for anything.

The first thing we did was to strip the space of the furniture and objects, creating a blank canvas to work from. With the clutter gone, it looked much bigger, and we could see possibilities that weren't there before. Starting from zero allows you to make deliberate choices about what the space should include.

Before moving anything back, we asked, "What's the purpose of this piece of furniture or object?" If there was no clear answer, we threw it away or put it in storage bins. Every object takes up mental space. The intention there was to make the bins recede into the background so the space felt clear.

Our goal was not just to create a peaceful environment but also to keep it that way. The bins provided temporary storage for things that needed a home. Once a month Lena went through them to throw things away. Over time, she and the kids became more mindful about bringing items into the space.

I also recommended placing items that Lena used occasionally, such as supplies for knitting, on rolling carts to move them around more easily and make the space more flexible. We wanted to maximize the living area. Having mobile storage in corners or against the wall creates value for previously wasted space.

Resetting Objects

Many teachers create safe spaces in their classroom for children to go to when their emotions are running high. Teachers often put comforting objects in these corners to help children reset their emotions, such as books, puzzles, and quiet activities.

Similarly, you can add objects to your calm-down corner to promote mindfulness, breathing, and reflection, such as a journal or comforting memento. One simple thing I recommend you keep in this space is a cup of rice. When I facilitate an event that requires a high level of attention and energy, I often start by asking participants to sit on the floor and silently count rice grains. Imagine high-powered executives ready to engage in a day of creative work sitting on the floor and counting. It works. Counting rice doesn't require much energy or concentration, but it focuses the brain and creates space for reflection.

The ideal calm-down space has limited foot traffic, but the nook in Lena's home was part of her open-plan living room. She couldn't shut the door and have the space to herself. With two active boys underfoot, Lena needed to signal to them—and herself—when she was taking a break. For this, I recommended she add a signal gong. Whenever Lena enters her calm-down corner, she hits the flat, circular metal disk with a mallet. At first Lena felt self-conscious striking the gong. "It felt corny and beside the point. But I noticed the boys respected my space and didn't bother me when they heard the gong. Now I look forward to that deep, resonant sound. It's like a treat for my brain."

I discussed in a previous chapter how objects in a space come alive when a routine is attached to them (see Prepare Your Space for Activity, page 50). In Lena's case, the sound was both powerful and calming, signaling not just to others but also to her own brain that she was shifting gears.

Before you start designing your entire home for calm, start with one corner, incorporating the tips I've outlined in the previous pages. Creating a space where you can meditate, read, journal, or just be quiet with your thoughts is essential as our lives become more stressful and hectic. My friend Lena found her calm-down corner to be so essential to her mental health that she designed similar sanctuaries for her two boys. Now everyone in the household has a designated area in which nothing is required of them and that is theirs and theirs alone.

EMBRACE
IMPERFECTION

Like many designers, I enjoy starting new things (and those don't always have to be start-ups). A few years ago, I was taking a break from writing a graphic novel about Ukraine, a project I started with a wonderful British illustrator. This was an important personal endeavor because I'm originally from Ukraine and have wanted to share immigrant experiences for quite some time. For this mini-break, I decided to go on a ten-day trek in the Himalayas, which I'd never done before and thought was a great idea.

Little did I know before I started on that journey that on the first day, we would have to fire our sherpa because he didn't know his way. Midway through the trip, it started to rain. What happens in the mountains when it rains? Leeches! Every evening after a long hike, I would have to pull bloodsuckers off my legs that had crawled up my shoes and pant legs toward my flesh. Many more unexpected experiences like this one, big and small, happened along the way.

On the last day of the trip, our small group came upon a mountain hut where a sheepherder slept, surrounded by his sheep. He welcomed us by setting up a fire and treated us to some tea and caterpillar fungus. At night when I stepped out of the hut, I saw what seemed like a thousand sheep staring back at me with their eyes glowing in the dark. We had finally reached our destination—the glacier. I remember that moment vividly. I also remember every failure on that trek.

Throw Away the Failure
But Keep the Lesson

After graduating from Stanford University, I worked at the Stanford Technology Ventures Program for a fabulous woman, Professor Tina Seelig, who encouraged her students to write a failure resume. In her book, *What I Wish I Knew When I Was 20: A Crash Course on Finding Your Place in the World*, Tina describes the importance of acknowledging and reflecting on your failures as much as on your successes as a way of advancing forward.

In Silicon Valley, failure is considered a good thing for serial entrepreneurs. In fact, the new wave of entrepreneurs I've collaborated with and mentored embraces failing fast, failing often, and failing forward as a way to journey toward success. One of the all-time favorite "failure" exercises the start-up founders I've met like to do is a Tear Me Down.

Tear Me Down

This exercise is very simple yet powerful. Take a piece of paper and fold it in half. On one side, write down your biggest project failure. On the other, write down what you've learned from it. Tear the piece of paper in half. Throw away the failure; keep the lesson. Wait for an opportunity to apply it, and then repeat. As you embark on your space redesign project, keep track of failures and key lessons along the way, so you can incorporate and iterate upon them in the future. This makes for a good iterative design practice you can develop over time.

Golden Repair

Another thing to remember as you create a calmer environment is that it's extremely rare to arrive at a great outcome on the first try—it usually takes several iterations and improvements. A great example of this creative cycle comes from kintsukuroi, or kintsugi (golden repair), the Japanese art of repairing pottery with gold lacquer. The belief behind this art form is that a piece is more beautiful for having been broken. Keep a few "broken" or imperfect artifacts around in a designated area (like a treasure chest) as a reminder of past work.

At the Stanford d.school, there is a ritual of clearing the space at the end of the workday, even going so far as to bring out trash bins and toss prototypes that no longer are needed. You can create a ritual of cleaning up and resetting your space every evening. However, the goal of cleaning up and resetting is not to make your place pristine. Leave some visual reminders of the creative cycle and work that was done. This is the visual language of your space; not to mention, it's sometimes intimidating to start a creative endeavor if you're in clean room surrounded by whiteboards and blank sheets of paper.

ACTIVATE YOUR CALM

A few years ago, a close friend of twenty years invited me to her son's birthday party. It was a fun celebration held in a park near her house with the usual fare for kids and parents. I chatted with different moms for a while and was about to head out but was stopped by my friend. She wanted to introduce me to her rabbi and his wife, who had just arrived. Rabbi Shimon and his wife, Chanie, were so lovely, kind, and engaging that I ended up staying longer and having a conversation about what it means to have a good, kind home. Chanie shared a wealth of knowledge rooted in the rich four-thousand-year-old tradition of Judaism. It was so inspiring that we were the last ones to leave the party. On our way out, she said, "What are you doing next Friday? Come to Shabbat!" I agreed.

I had never been to Shabbat dinner at a rabbi's house before, so when I got home, I began to research what it meant and how it was done.

This traditional Friday night Jewish meal is held at sundown and has a specific set of dishes that are prepared ahead of time, as well as specific rules and rituals associated with it that have deep spiritual meaning. I won't share them all here, but two that immediately stood out to me as very appropriate to address some of the modern-day challenges of the fast-paced, stressful life we are living were lighting candles on a Friday night followed by a technology-free Saturday. But more on that shortly.

When I arrived at the rabbi's house the following week, I was greeted by two lovely, starry-eyed five-year-old girls that I later found out were one of three sets of twins! They took me to the dining room, where beautiful silver tableware was already set, candles were ready to be lit, and two loaves of freshly baked challah bread and a bottle of red kosher wine were on the table. I contributed a bouquet of flowers and some chocolate.

The Importance of Routine and Rituals

We began with lighting Shabbat candles, drawing the warmth of the fire toward us three times with the palms of our hands, followed by a short blessing. I found this moment to be so simple yet so profound; it didn't require anything but two tea lights, matches, and the intention of bringing joy and transcending from mundane daily life. Rabbi Shimon shared some wine after another blessing. We washed hands and tasted yummy challah. Next came the food, and what a feast it was! Multiple courses included various salads and appetizers, fish, soup, chicken, dessert, and more—all lovingly prepared by Chanie and her daughters.

During dinner, Chanie shared her family fish recipe and told us a story that came along with it. Before marinating and baking a fish, her grandmother cut off the head instead of keeping the fish whole. Her recipe and this way of cooking were passed on through three generations until one day, her granddaughter asked why she cut off the fish head. To Chanie's surprise, grandma revealed that back in the day, she only had one roasting pan of a certain length and the fish she was baking often wouldn't fit, so she just cut off the head to make it work. In the end, this wasn't some "secret sauce" in the preparation that made it taste great. It reminded me of how we often try to fit into our space instead of having our space fit us and support our creative spirit.

After a great deal of eating, talking, and laughing came rest. Rabbi Shimon shared that on Shabbat, it is customary to rest, read, and play with kids—no work is allowed, including using technology, such as phones and computers. *What a wonderful tech-detox idea!* I thought.

Most of us know that even outside of work responsibilities, we spend too much time on our devices, and research certainly confirms it. For instance, one study using 2011–2012 survey results from the Center for Disease Control found that those who spend six hours or more per day watching screens had a higher risk for depression, and another found that limiting social media use to thirty minutes per day led to a "significant improvement in well-being." Experts say adults should limit screen time outside of work to less than two hours per day. The type and quality of screen time also plays a role. Similarly, for kids the recommendation is to limit screen time to thirty minutes or less per day.

Shabbat, I thought, provided a wonderful opportunity for the family to cut down on screen time, feel more present, and connect with each other in person. I left the rabbi's house uplifted and inspired to incorporate this practice in my household. The reason I'm sharing this story with you is to illustrate how being intentional about building out your repertoire of artifacts, routines, and cadences can help transform your space into a sanctuary.

To activate your calm through calming objects and routines, begin by writing out your typical weekly patterns—for example, things you do every morning or at the end of a work week. Look for recurring moments or transitions that could be supported with small rituals. For instance, perhaps you have a cup of tea to center yourself before work each morning, so you set up a small tea station with your favorite mugs and tea accessories. Or you light candles in the dining room every Friday night before dinner as a way of introducing calm at the end of the workweek. Keeping tea lights in that area will serve as an easy visual cue for this transition into the weekend.

You can move from room to room to either identify any existing rituals you have that activate your calm or imagine some new ones you might have discovered in this book. Consider writing down each ritual and its cadence (daily, weekly, or monthly) in your journal or planner so that these small moments become part of your established routine.

In Hebrew, there is a saying: "Shinui makom, shinui mazal," which means "Change your environment, change your luck." I wish for you to be the master of your place and change your surroundings (and luck) for the better.

I would like to thank my literary agent, Lynn Jones Johnston, who spent countless hours crafting the book proposal with me and managed to meet up with me in person in NYC right before the pandemic started. I'd also like to thank a fantastic publishing team from Chronicle Books: wonderful and patient editors Rachel Hiles and Magnolia Molcan, editorial director Sarah Billingsley, and multitalented book designer Vanessa Dina.

My family has been instrumental in making this project happen by relentlessly supporting my dreams and aspirations, so big thanks to my mom, Luda, my daughter, Lily, and my uncle, Remi (and in remembrance of my father, Nick). I would also like to wholeheartedly acknowledge my friends whose personal stories and journeys inspired this book: Mary Dotter, Karl Dotter, Katrina Child,

Lena Ostrovskaya and her family, Shimon and Chanie Gruzman, Dovid and Shulamis Labkowski, Lynn Michiko Powers, Svetlana Royzen, Vera Fainshtein, Olga Zilberbourg, Kristin Scheel, Josey Mulberry, Nicole Mercado, Liz Walsh, Mary Samson, Myleen Hollero, Sirima Sataman, Beth Lee Sanzone, Pireeni Sundaralingam, Dilruba Ahmed, Cristina Bowerman, Kay Mercado, and many others.

Thank you to my former classmates, professors, and colleagues from Stanford University who continue to influence and educate me in myriad ways: Adam Royalty, Scott Witthoft, Rich Crandall, Jim Ratcliffe, Maryanna Rogers, Charlotte Burgess-Auburn, George Kembel, Daniel Stringer, Ben Grossman-Kahn, Meg Lee Weir, Molly Claire Wilson, Leticia Britos Cavagnaro, Scott Doorley, Erica Estrada-Liou, Kerry O'Connor,

Sarah Stein Greenberg, Susie Wise, Tina Seelig, Bernie Roth, Fred Leichter, Shelley Goldman, Lee Shulman, Cheryl Richardson, Desiree Pointer Mace, Anne Lieberman, Esther Wojcicki, and David Kelley. Thank you to the design and innovation colleagues who are my role models and have shown tremendous support and inspiration throughout the years: Sandy Speicher, Marinus Vandenberg, Kim Caruana, Kiran Bir Sethi, Beti Cung, Diana Joseph, Debbie Brackeen, and many others. Thank you!